Table of Contents

Foreword

September 2018, Dundee, Scotland: we've just moved in together into a tiny flat after only knowing each other vaguely through the comics industry. Three years later, we now live in different countries and have grown into our trans identities - out and proud, and all that entails.

Transgender people often share key milestones - getting a meaningful haircut, choosing our name, putting on an outfit that makes us feel like ourselves - but we also go though our own individual, highly personal journeys. We are a community that can find comfort in our similarities and strength in our differences.

Narratives around us centre the idea that *dysphoria* is the thing that makes us trans; that our identities are rooted in conflict between our bodies, our minds, and society. But rarely is the spotlight shone on the joys, the *euphoria* of being who we are.

Even though it was our focus going into this book, we were still surprised by how often euphoria can be found in seemingly unrelated parts of a trans person's life. Being trans touches every aspect of your existence and brings us happiness in the most unexpected ways.

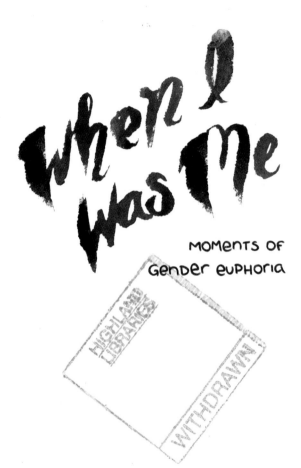

When I Was Me

Moments of Gender Euphoria

edited by
Eve Greenwood & Alex Assan

book design by
Spire Eaton

Whether this book teaches you a little more about
a topic you weren't familiar with, or you draw comfort
from the stories within; whether it helps you understand
yourself better, or it helps someone else understand *you*;
even if it only gives you a little smile, we truly hope you
enjoy your read.

Thank you to all the contributors who took the time to
share their stories and artwork with us, and thank you to
those in our contributors' lives who made these chosen
moments special. Thank you to everyone who supported
this project. And lastly, thank you to our own families,
friends, and communities, who always bring us joy.

- Eve & Alex

Memory

when deep in the landfill

the servers awake

to weird noises

Amanda Castillo
amanda-castillo.com
@mandallin

Amanda is a comic artist and illustrator from the Bay Area who loves to tell heartfelt stories inspired by the people and world around them.

BACK IN THE EARLY DAYS OF 2000'S INTERNET, I USED TO HANG OUT ON NEOPETS A LOT.

PARTICULARLY THEIR FORUMS.

Ang Hui Qing
o_O
36 Months
Unknown

I ENJOYED THAT MY GENDER DIDN'T NEED TO BE PART OF ANYTHING.

I HADN'T THOUGHT ABOUT NEOPETS IN A LONG WHILE.

BITCH BOY. WHAT ARE YOU UP TO?

MY LOVE. JUST ABOUT TO MAKE DINNER.

HUI QING AND I ARE HAVING A DEBATE.

EDIE. HELP. THEY SAY SEAHORSES AREN'T FISH.

IS HQ GOOD WITH THAT?

I'LL CHECK WITH THEM.

THEY SAY BREAD IS BORING.

TELL THEM THEY'RE WRONG.

I LOVE THEM DESPITE THEIR DERANGED OPINIONS.

"THEY" FEELS LIKE LITTLE FIREWORKS EVERY TIME.

I DIDN'T HAVE THE WORDS FOR IT BACK THEN BUT "UNKNOWN" WAS THE CLOSEST I COULD GET TO DESCRIBING MY SENSE OF SELF.

IT'S WONDERFUL HOW BITS OF MY PAST MAKE MORE SENSE NOW I HAVE BETTER WORDS FOR IT.

Ang Hui Qing
anghuiqing.com
🐦 @BurdHQ

they

Ang Hui Qing is an illustrator and concept artist from Malaysia. Their art seeks to explore the fantastical in the mundane, and the mundane in the fantastical.

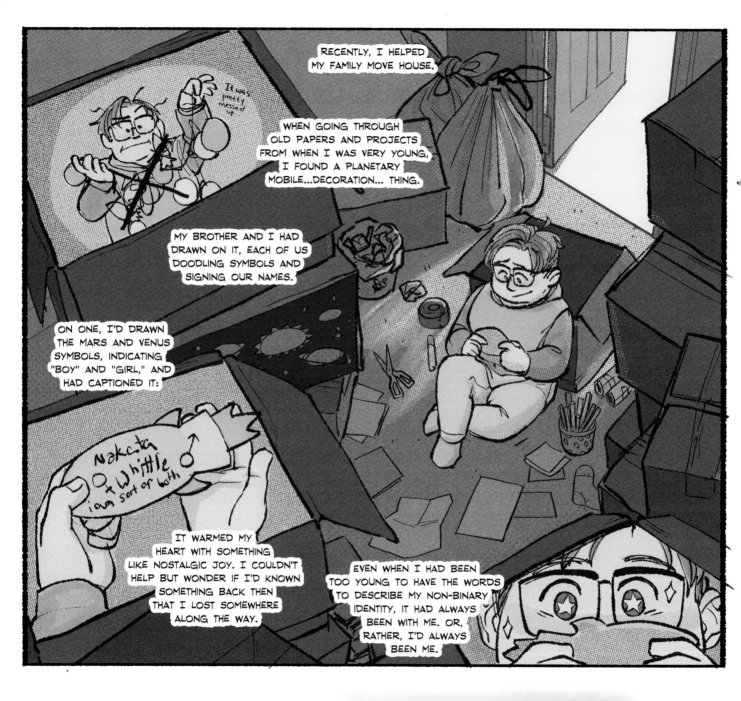

Knack Whittle
nakatawhittle.weebly.com
🐦 @whittledraws

Knack is a cartoonist and sequential artist living on the US east coast who enjoys buff women, queer media, and vampires (ideally all at once).

My gender-fluidity is best expressed when I am having fun with how I dress.

It's something I joyfully explore.

But it took finding a pirate amongst princesses

to remind me I've always been this way,

and always will be!

Filipa Estrela
feltmythical.com
🐦 @fylisfe

any pro nouns

Filipa loves making crafts, comics, and costumes. They are a queer dork whose stories draw from their mixed heritage and blend the everyday with magic.

St. Patrick's School · 2nd Grade

Jaime Dear
deardearjai.me
🐦 @DearDearJaime

Jaime Dear is a dirt poet, book designer, zinester, and comic artist from Ohio. You can find *Pivot*, their queer softball comic, online.

WHEN I WAS IN ELEMENTARY SCHOOL, BEFORE I KNEW WHAT BEING TRANS WAS, I USED TO WRITE A LOT OF COMICS INVOLVING PEOPLE "CROSSDRESSING".

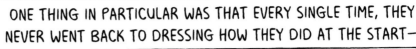

ONE THING IN PARTICULAR WAS THAT EVERY SINGLE TIME, THEY NEVER WENT BACK TO DRESSING HOW THEY DID AT THE START—

PEOPLE AROUND THEM WOULD ACCEPT THEM,

AND SOMETIMES THEY WOULD EVEN FIND LOVE.

I COMPLETELY FORGOT ABOUT IT FOR MORE THAN A DECADE, BUT NOW THAT IT HAS ALL COME BACK, IT MAKES A LOT OF SENSE IN HINDSIGHT.

Repressed memory

BAPOGICHI
🐦 @tagasaing

 he

BAPOGICHI is a comic artist based in Metro Manila who makes comics and illustrations mostly about trans characters.

Val Wise
valkwise.com
🐦 @valkwise

he

Val Wise is a comic artist based in the Southern US. He contributed to *Rolled & Told*, *Wayward Kindred*, and illustrated *Cheer Up! Love and Pompoms*.

hesitantdoodle
hesitantdoodle.com
@hesitantdoodle

they

hesitantdoodle is a non-binary Scottish illustrator. Their work focuses on queer stories and characters with elements of action and comedy.

Discovery

diligent winds

drop their trade

to ask where

they're going

Sfé R. Monster
sfemonster.com
🐦 @sfemonster

they

Sfé is a trans and queer award-winning Canadian comic maker, creating stories about monsters, mayhem, and magic.

Steve Stivaktis
@stivaktis

he
they

Steve is a trans comic artist and illustrator based in Athens, Greece, who particularly enjoys telling fun queer stories and filling the world with stickers.

THIS IS A STORY FROM BEFORE I REALISED I WAS TRANS...

ABOUT THE BEST BIRTHDAY PRESENT I HAVE EVER RECEIVED!

MY WIFE (THEN GIRLFRIEND) GOT ME SOME BRAS AND SOME BREASTFORMS.

BUT TO GET THE BRAS, SHE HAD TO GO TO A LINGERIE STORE.

SHE WAS NERVOUS AND NEEDED TO ASK FOR HELP.

I WANT TO GET SOMETHING FOR MY GIRLFRIEND...

SHE CALLED ME HER GIRLFRIEND FOR CONVENIENCE.

BUT I...

DON'T KNOW HER SIZE.

NO PROBLEM!

WHAT CUP SIZE DO YOU THINK SHE IS?

FOR SOME REASON THAT I COULDN'T EXPLAIN, BEING CALLED HER GIRLFRIEND MADE ME REALLY HAPPY!

Luna Grey
behance.net/lunathomas
@ @lunagreyart

 she

Luna spends most of her time working on her PhD (on stag beetles) or drawing comics. She also loves to bake, ride her bike and go on dates with her wife.

FINDING WORDS TO EXPLAIN HOW I FEEL ABOUT WHO I AM HAS BEEN ONE OF THE LONGEST JOURNEYS I'VE EVER BEEN ON.

I WAS 27 WHEN I HEARD A POEM MY MUSIC APP RECOMMENDED TO ME CALLED "YOUR LIFE" BY A GENDERQUEER ARTIST CALLED ANDREA GIBSON

THE POEM LAID OUT SO ELOQUENTLY EVERYTHING ABOUT HOW I HAD BEEN FEELING TOO, IN A WAY THAT FINALLY CONNECTED WITH ME.

AND SUDDENLY I MADE SENSE.

Cat Laird
catrionalaird.co.uk
🐦 @owlroostart

they

Cat is a freelance illustrator, comic artist and writer based in Scotland, creating stories to inspire hope and joy for those who need them.

20:16:02 WilyWolf: I just thought we should chat ;)
20:16:18 WilyWolf cuddles up :3
20:16:30 WilyWolf: Maybe we could get to know each other a little?
20:16:42   Me: Oh um, hello!
20:16:48 WilyWolf: Hehe, you are cute when you're shy ^_^

why does this feel so

20:19:18 WilyWolf: Oh god, I'm sorry, I really thought you were a w
20:19:22   Me: It's okay!
20:19:45   Me: I kind of liked it...?
20:19:58 WilyWolf: Well good I guess ^_^
20:20:04   Me: Is that weird?
20:20:11 WilyWolf: I don't know, I'm just glad you aren't mad ~_~

Kimball Anderson
outside-life.com

Kimball's art probes at the parts of ourselves
that we judge as not enough or too ambiguous,
honouring their meaning and beauty.

Dodo
𝐭 @dodoseraphim

any pro nouns

Dodo is an animator and comic artist passionate about creating stories filled with whimsy and joy.

Exploration

ruminant mountains

are steadily making

new choices

IT WAS THE MOST BEAUTIFUL DREAM I EVER HAD

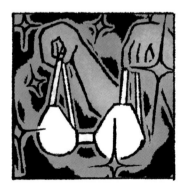
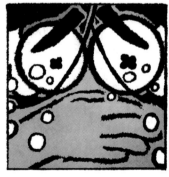

Guist
 @gui5t_

she

I go by Guist online but my friends call me Anne.
I'm a French animation student at Gobelins who likes
niche things nobody should ever ever care about.

OVOE WAS THE FIRST NONBINARY CHARACTER I MADE FOR A TABLETOP CAMPAIGN

OVOE USES THEY PRONOUNS

WOW I LOVE **THEM**

THE MORE MY FELLOW PLAYERS VALIDATED THEM THE STRONGER MY OWN THEY/THEM EUPHORIA BECAME

SO...

I... THINK I MIGHT GO BY "**THEY**" TOO.

Winter J. Kiakas
jkiakas.com
🐦 @winterjaykiakas

they

Winter Jay is a storyteller from Montreal who spends their time playing tabletop and creating stories with their partner that they eventually turn into books.

One day fairly early into my transition, I went out to walk my dog.

It was a regular Friday morning.

When I exited the lift, I caught a glimpse of a woman looking at me.

For a brief moment, I thought it must have been a neighbour I hadn't met yet.

It was me.

Tamar

she

Tamar is a queer Israeli girl who loves computers, biology, chess and hiking in the beautiful nature around her.

art by
Noah Schiatti
(pg 91)

WHEN I DECIDED TO CHANGE MY NAME

I DREAMT ABOUT IT.

OF HOW IT WOULD MAKE ME FEEL: HOW MY FRIENDS WOULD ACCEPT IT.

WHEN I WOKE UP, I STARED AT MYSELF IN THE MIRROR AND REPEATED MY CHOSEN NAME OVER AND OVER.

MY FRIENDS SPENT HOURS LOOKING THROUGH BABY NAME SITES WITH ME, ADVISING AND ENCOURAGING.

IT WAS IMPORTANT TO ME...

THAT THE NAME BE PRONOUNCEABLE IN MY MOTHER TONGUE.

AND THEN I HAPPENED UPON THE NAME I WAS CONSIDERING FOR THE FIRST TIME IN A BOOK BY A COLOMBIAN POET.

JAIME MANRIQUE
EMINENT MARICONES

Jaime

AND SO I FOUND A NAME I CONNECTED TO EMOTIONALLY AND TO MY COLOMBIAN BACKGROUND...

AND I STILL FEEL THE SHOCK OF EUPHORIA EVERY TIME SOMEONE SAYS MY NAME.

Jaime Mosquera
elsombreronart.com
🐦 @elsombreronart

Jaime Mosquera is a Latine comics artist who focuses on horror and phantasmagoria. They love stories about lesbian vampires and gothic romance.

I saw it there on every visit to the arcade, but I was nowhere near brave enough to try it out.

Hey, I'm gonna go play *DDR* or something I'll be back later.

OK, cool!

I was scared. It wasn't an empty arcade. People would see me.

It was just for fun though... Right?

Afraid to dance, I kept my fists closed at first, punching at the arrow prompts.

But the avatar began influencing my motions. My hands began to open...

A hidden spark inside my heart sang. Her preview duet with freedom.

Amy-Lynn Greig
🐦 @defaultprincess

An ephemeral being always somewhere between a sunbathed floral greenhouse, and a nighttime café playing faded City Pop.

Spire Eaton
spiremint.carbonmade.com
🐦 @spiremint

Spire draws the webcomic *Recoil*. His hobbies include thinking about boys and critter spotting.

Hari Conner
hari-illustration.com
 they
🐦 @haridraws

Hari is a transmasc fantasy dweeb and hopeless
forest romantic. You can read their award winning
webcomic *Finding Home* on the internet.

Presentation

the screens

crack up citywide

with the stories

they're showing

I ALREADY HAD A SCHEDULE FOR MY GRAD PHOTOSHOOT WHEN LOCKDOWN STARTED.

MAR 2020

OBVIOUSLY IT DIDN'T PUSH THROUGH, BUT I STILL NEEDED ONE FOR MY ONLINE CEREMONY.

FOR YEARS, I'D DREAMED OF WEARING A BARONG FOR MY GRADUATION.

← traditional, formal menswear, worn at weddings, etc.

I HAD JUST ASSUMED I'D GET AROUND TO BUYING MY OWN WHEN THE TIME CAME, BUT...

INSTEAD, I BORROWED MY BROTHER'S OVERSIZED BARONG.

WE DID THE SHOOT AT HOME.

IT WAS MY FIRST TIME WEARING ONE.

I DON'T THINK I'LL EVER FORGET THE JOY OF IT.

ESPECIALLY BECAUSE OF HOW IMPERFECT THE CIRCUMSTANCES WERE.

Gillian Pascasio (7CLUBS)
7clubsart.carrd.co
🐦 @7GROVEYS

7CLUBS is a Filipino tibo/bigender character and comic artist. She loves to make stories about LGBT+ joy, love, and dragons.

Maxine Frizz
grizzlymittz.com
@ @grizzlymittz

Just a frizzy-headed lass that likes to make people laugh and feel things. My interests include robots, cute stuff, retro games, and not being on fire.

Lio Pressland
kroov.club
🐦 @kroovv

he they

I'm Lio AKA kroov, a comic artist and illustrator from Scotland. I love fantasy, D&D and making far too many OCs.

Blue

he

Blue is a Scottish trans man who never grew out of his emo phase. He befriends every cat he sees, despite having a menagerie of animals at home.

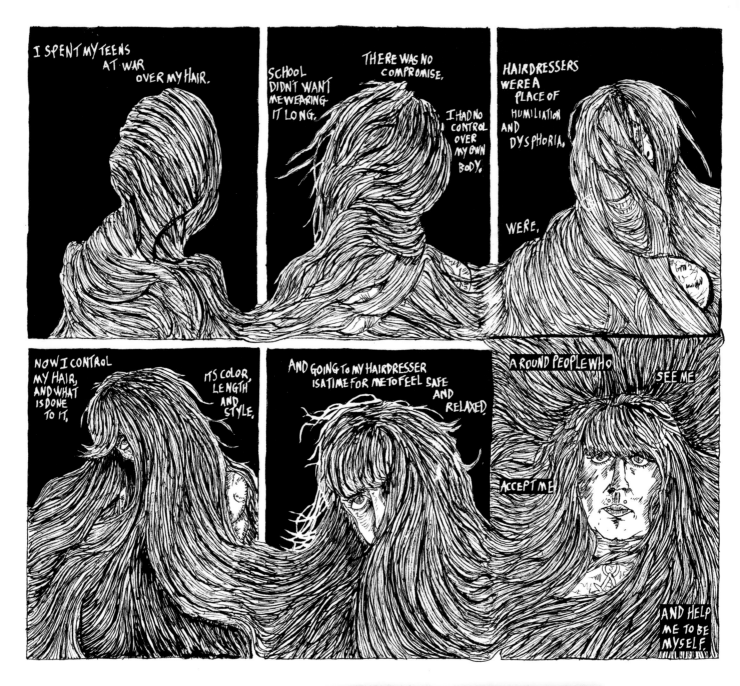

Erika Price
🐦 @erikapriceart

Erika Price is a comic artist based in the UK. She is known for her horror comics.

FOR A LONG TIME, I FELT THAT HAVING LONG HAIR WOULD BEST EXPRESS MY GENDER IDENTITY. MAYBE EVEN ALLOW ME TO "PASS".

BUT SOME TIME INTO MY TRANSITION, I WANTED TO TRY A SHORTER STYLE.

I WAS NERVOUS ABOUT IT BUT MY HAIRDRESSER (WHO WAS ALSO TRANS) REASSURED ME.

THE MOMENT I LOOKED IN THE MIRROR AND SAW MYSELF...

...MY DOUBTS FADED AWAY.

IT FELT RIGHT.

Peleg Bar Lev

they

I'm 24 and live in Ramat Gan, Israel with my cat Waffle. I'm a mathematics graduate student, a trans activist, and a roleplayer.

art by
Blop
(pg 91)

I WAS WALKING DOWN AGRIPAS STREET IN JERUSALEM, WHERE I USED TO LIVE BEFORE MY TRANSITION.

WHENEVER I WALKED THERE IN THE PAST, RELIGIOUS MEN WOULD OFTEN ASK ME TO LAY *TEFILLIN* – A PRACTICE ONLY MEN ARE TRADITIONALLY ALLOWED TO PARTAKE IN.

THAT DAY, I SAW A MAN STANDING FURTHER DOWN THE ROAD AND WORRIED THAT HE WOULD APPROACH ME.

INSTEAD, WHEN I PASSED HIM, I HEARD A WOMAN'S VOICE CALLING TO ME.

CAN I OFFER YOU SHABBAT CANDLES, MISS?

Rotem Sorek

she

I'm a trans activist, doing work for Hoshen and IGY (two of Israel's LGBT organisations). I'm an avid reader of fantasy and sci-fi, and a piano player.

art by
Rowan Oats
(pg 91)

GalacticJonah
galacticjonah.com
🐦 @galacticjonah

he

Trans man and freelance artist based in Switzerland.
Loves illustration, character design and TTRPGs.

I'VE ALWAYS LIKED MY HANDS. A PIECE OF MYSELF DEVOID OF GENDER.

THEY'RE NOT PERFECT.

I HAVE CALLUSES ON MY FINGERS.

THE BONES OF MY PINKY ARE CROOKED.

I HAVE SCARS ATOP MY HANDS.

BUT THESE THINGS TELL STORIES ABOUT ME.

ANY ARTIST KNOWS HOW PRECIOUS OUR HANDS ARE.

POWERFUL TOOLS FOR CREATION AND SELF EXPRESSION.

I CRAFTED MYSELF INTO WHO I AM.

I HAD TO LEARN HOW TO SPEAK AGAIN AS MY VOICE CRACKED FOR MONTHS.

IT WAS GREAT, THEY WERE JOYFUL SOUNDS.

ONE THING THAT SURPRISED ME THE MOST WAS HOW THE HAIRS FROM MY ARMS NOW STRETCH DOWN TO THE TOPS OF MY HANDS.

THIS CHANGE WAS UNEXPECTED. I NEVER SAW ANYONE TALK ABOUT LITTLE THINGS LIKE THAT.

A BEAUTIFUL PIECE OF ME.

Kale de Wild
kalesbug.com
🐦 @_KalesBug

they

I work in comics and animation but my true passion is making silly little men dance and kiss for my entertainment.

I CAME OUT DURING COVID-19, WHEN I WAS FEELING REALY ISOLATED.

SOMEHOW, I STARTED SWAPPING SELFIES WITH OTHER TRANS PEOPLE I KNEW.

AND EVEN SOME FRIENDS WHO WERE DOING SOME EXPLORING.

THERE IS A SPECIAL KIND OF INTIMACY TO THIS PRACTICE, I THINK.

AND A SORT OF MAGIC TO THE PICTURES THEMSELVES. A BOLDNESS.

THEY'RE BEAUTIFUL.

Alex Assan
alexassanart.com
🐦 @alexassanart

he they

Alex is a comic artist from Tel Aviv who loves romance, historical fiction and musical theatre. He works with trans youth and has a big beautiful dog.

Acceptance

circles of well-dressed stones

make troubling findings

AS A TRANS AND FILIPINO—AMERICAN PERSON,

MY IDENTITY HAD ALWAYS LEFT ME FEELING LIKE I WAS DESPERATELY TRYING TO MIX OIL AND WATER.

I HAD CONSTANTLY FELT SEPARATE FROM MYSELF— NEVER COMPLETE OR WHOLE.

IT WAS NOT UNTIIL I FULLY CAME TO TERMS WITH MY TRANSNESS THAT I REALISED I WAS NEVER A SPLIT BEING.

WITH TESTOSTERONE AS THE HYDROGEN BOND IN MY DNA,

IT TOOK TRANSITIONING FOR ME TO REALIZE THAT

I HAVE ALWAYS BEEN WHOLE.

Apollo Baltazar
pmbaltazar.myportfolio.com
🐦 @pm_baltazar

he they

Apollo is a cartoonist born in Southern California currently pursuing their BFA in Cartooning. They love romance novels and writing letters to their friends.

IT DOESN'T
FEEL LIKE A HUGE
COINCIDENCE

THAT
I GREW CLOSER TO SO
MANY OF THE PEOPLE
I CARE ABOUT

AFTER
FIGURING
OUT WHO I WAS
IN THE FIRST
PLACE

Ashley Caswell
ashleycaswell.com
@caswell_ashley

they

Ashley is a nonbinary illustrator, book designer, and comic artist living in Brooklyn. Their work often explores love, anxiety and growth with a unique sense of humour.

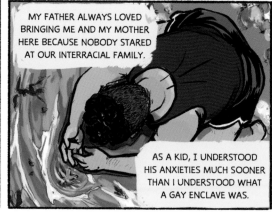

Adam Green
behance.net/adamgreen_
🐦 @Glittertooth

A while back I had the epiphany that I could transition instead of living vicariously through my art. I don't know why I didn't think of that sooner.

Otava Heikkilä
🐦 @claystorks
he

Otava is from Tampere, Finland, creating comics for queer adult audiences about whatever beautiful and sordid is occupying his mind at the moment.

BEFORE ACCEPTING MYSELF, I FOUND IT HARD TO BE IN PUBLIC.

IT WASN'T UNTIL I STARTED SURROUNDING MYSELF WITH OTHER QUEER PEOPLE THAT I WAS ABLE TO ACCEPT MY OWN IDENTITY AND FEEL SO MUCH MORE CONFIDENT IN MY OWN SKIN.

IT MADE ME REALISE THERE'S NO ONE WAY TO BE QUEER.

I DIDN'T CARE HOW PEOPLE PERCEIVED ME ANYMORE. I COULD LOOK HOWEVER I WANTED.

Ribbons

they

Ribbons is a young person from Scotland who enjoys music, crochet and anything that is bright and colourful!

art by
Jae Zander Kitinoja
(pg 91)

BaronBoar
baronboar.carrd.co
🐦 @BaronBoar

he
they

Griffin is an artist from rural Aberdeenshire, with a love for the natural world and its beasts. His work puts them in the forefront of fantasy and horror.

Community

couplets and triplets

grow strange in the heat

of their knowing

I LOOK A CERTAIN WAY. A WAY THAT MEANS I HAVE TO COMPROMISE WITH HOW I FEEL VS HOW I'M PERCEIVED.

BUT WHEN I'M WITH MY FRIENDS, IT DOESN'T MATTER WHAT MY BODY LOOKS LIKE.

THEY UNDERSTAND MY GENDER, THEY SEE ME FOR WHO I AM, AND MAN—

MAN!

I FEEL LIKE A WOMAN.

IT FEELS AMAZING.

Eve Greenwood
evegwood.com
🐦 @evegwood

they

Eve is a nonbinary comic creator from Scotland who loves languages, both real and fake. They create the webcomic *Inhibit* and make it everyone's problem.

I HAD NEVER HEARD MY NAME

AND HAD NEVER BEEN GRACED WITH GIRL-HOOD BEFORE...

A TUMBLR MEET-UP ORGANISED BY FLIP-PHONE.

AN OUTFIT THAT SCREAMED "TEENAGE BOY."

WHO COULD BELIEVE I WAS ANYTHING MORE?

THERE SHE IS!

IT'S WINONA!!

HEY...

THAT'S ME!

Winona Powers
bit.ly/winpowers
▶ @vanillavial

she

Winona Powers is a comic artist and animator who spent her childhood years dreaming of making cartoons and becoming a girl. Now her body of work is as trans as the body she inhabits.

I remember sitting in the library of my university back in first year. I was on the third floor, trying to escape the noise of campus.

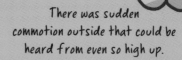

There was sudden commotion outside that could be heard from even so high up.

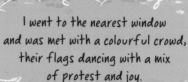

I went to the nearest window and was met with a colourful crowd, their flags dancing with a mix of protest and joy.

BUT IT'S OCTOBER!

ISN'T PRIDE IN JUNE?

I learned shortly after that South Africans often celebrate pride month in October, when the first pride march was held in South Africa (and the African continent!) in 1990.

It's this history and the resilience of LGBTQ+ voices that continue to exist in this country, in big ways and small, that give me the courage to be who I am every day.

Noel Fox
🐦 @hexed_boy

he they

Hi I'm Noel! I'm an independent artist from South Africa who loves to draw cute and spooky things!

When I was growing up, I didn't know what transgender was.

There were no transgender people in my everyday life or on TV. It felt like my life was in black and white.

After doing research on my own, I realised I was transgender.

It felt like my life had colour again.

Now my life goal is to bring that colour to the lives of other transgender people ...

...and be that person they can talk to who makes them realise they are not alone.

C-Jay Quigley
🐦 @CJayQuigley

 she

C-Jay is a transwoman from Glasgow who loves to play video games and read comics in her spare time. She is also an LGBTQ+ activist.

art by
Tori A. Rielly
(pg 91)

dairysam
dairysam.wixsite.com/portfolio
@ @dairy.sam

dairysam is a queer, disabled, brown artist from Toronto. They love playing with colours, shapes and characters to tell stories.

Fanfi
fanficciera.weebly.com
🐦 @estroboscopios

Fanfi is based in Chile. He has a multidisciplinary background in Fine Arts and focuses on erotic and sensual art in queer and trans contexts.

Family

nothing's as queer

or as true as

a theory unwinding

In 2016, my wife and I went to live with her grandmother, recently diagnosed with dementia, to be her full-time caretakers.

I love it!

At the time, I wasn't out as a trans man yet, and I was just testing the ground on presenting in a more masculine way.

Dona Carmem, who had known me for years already, took this wonderfully and was particularly gleeful in gifting me a neverending amount of boxers.

Silly boy...

As her disease progressed, she slowly started to forget I had ever presented as a woman.

Me?

Him!

She was the second person, after my wife, to refer to me almost exclusively with masculine pronouns.

Your bf

Yes, my bf

She never forgot me. She knew who I was —her granddaughter's spouse—until the very end.

What will always amuse me is that, when she started to require specialised help, her uncanny awareness started to spread around.

And I became every elderly man's missing grandson.

Tariq, Tariq, come help me, my son!

Dante Luiz
danteluiz.com
🐦 @dntlz

he

Dante Luiz is an illustrator and occasional writer from Brazil. He was published in several comic anthologies, and did the interior art for CREMA (comiXology/Dark Horse).

AFTER I CAME OUT, I THOUGHT THAT BEING TRANS WAS SOMETHING PEOPLE WOULD, AT BEST, UNDERSTAND AND TOLERATE.

BUT ON MY BIRTHDAY THAT YEAR I REALISED

MY TRANSNESS CAN BE **CHERISHED,**

CELEBRATED,

AND **LOVED.**

IT WAS THE SWEETEST SURPRISE OF ALL.

Ella Cesari
ellacesari.weebly.com
@drawnwithoutref

 she

Ella is an animator, story artist and cartoonist. She loves creating stories, as well as playing ukulele, wearing cute outfits, and bursting into song.

Simon K
dishsoapaddict.journoportfolio.com
@dishsoapaddict

Simon is a uni student who wants to pursue art as his career. He loves cartoons, Pixar movies, Krave cereal, and drawing 24/7.

Morgan Mei
meilianhoe.com
🐦 @Meiidiocre

Morgan is a queer storyboard and comic artist from Malaysia. They have a strange sense of humour best seen in their webcomic *My Husband is a Cultist*.

Jey Pawlik
jpawlik.com
🐦 @jeypawlik

Jey is a trans/nonbinary comic artist. They draw webcomics for Topaz Comics and their mission is to make exclusively queer comics for anyone to enjoy.

Intimacy

held in the kinship of

ragged and rude-soft voices

Jua OK!
juaok.com
@Jua.ok

 he they

Jua is an illustrator and comic artist whose work explores themes of queer identity, mental illness and relationships using bright colours and fluid line work.

Rhael McGregor
rhaelmcgregor.com
@ @raysdrawlings

Rhael McGregor is a Non-Binary/Two-Spirit Métis comic artist and animator from Winnipeg, Manitoba. They love to write stories that make people smile!

Ian Pinkis
behance.net/IanPinkis
@ianpinkisart

I'm an illustrator from Spain with a fluid style who loves drawing plants and warm colours.

Jade 'Jude' Sarson
teahermit.co.uk
🐦 @jadedlyco

Jade is an award-winning illustrator and comic artist. They like tea, big dogs and gut-punchingly passionate romance - as seen in their most well-known comics *Cafe Suada* and *For the Love of God, Marie!*.

Freedom

the easy

and free-tongued choir

of the earth

and its minding

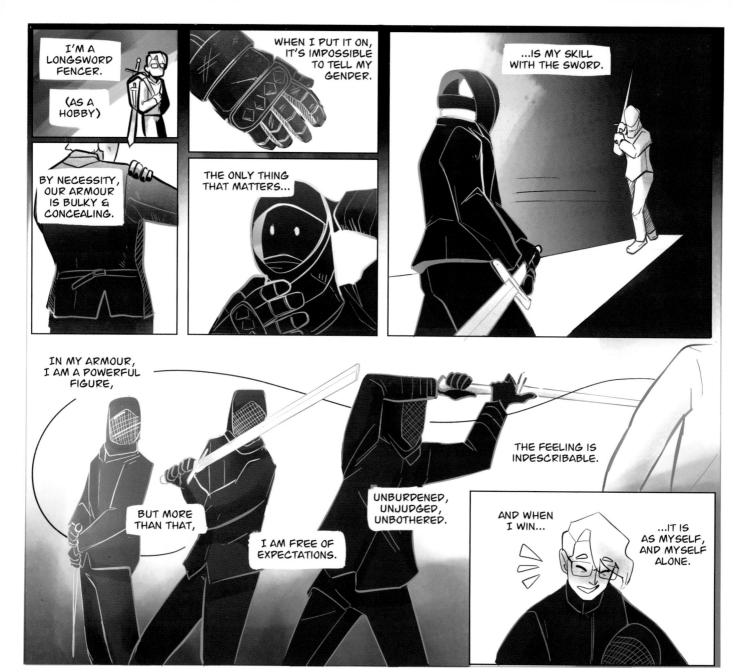

Noelle Hepworth
noellehepworth.com
@ @crisanonymous

Noelle is an innovative illustrator and sequential artist. Their work resonates with the human experience while subverting expectations with a dash of humour.

A few years ago, I agreed to join a pole dancing class with two cis girl friends.

You wear very little clothes to do this sport (bare skin grips best), so all my curves were out.

I felt uncomfortable – I wrestle with being perceived as female, or even feminine.

Unexpectedly, being around all kinds of unclothed bodies made me less self-conscious about my own. Pole class was even the first place I felt comfortable baring my unshaved legs.

Over time, building up muscle and learning to do tricks made me feel strong, brave.

Gratitude and pride about what my body did largely took the place of resentment about how it looked.

I don't want to stop doing ostensibly feminine things or hide my body's curves – I am queer, therefore whatever I do and look like is queer.

That makes me feel strong and brave, too.

G.C. Houle
gchoule.com
🐦 @gchoule

they

G.C. is a French-Canadian comic artist and graphic designer. They love to tell funny, feel-good stories about queer people, in every sense of the word.

I'VE SANG "SURE ON THIS SHINING NIGHT" BY MORTEN LAURIDSEN THREE DIFFERENT TIMES, IN THREE DIFFERENT VOCAL SECTIONS.

FIRST, THE SOARING SOPRANO PART, JUST BEFORE I WOULD START TO SUSPECT THAT I MIGHT NOT BE A GIRL

SECOND, THE NOBLE TENOR PART, AS I WAS PARTIALLY OUT AND STRUGGLING BADLY

FINALLY, THE RICH BASS PART, FULLY AND JOYFULLY MYSELF

INCENDAVERY

Incendavery
incendavery.com
@ @incendavery

he
they

Incendavery's work focuses on gender, sexuality, and mental health. He is best known for his diary comics, in which he depicts himself as a purple crow.

Naomi Rubin
naomiyaki.com
@naomiyaki

she

I make comics, translate Japanese, and cook a lot.
I draw *Moonsprout Station* and have done work for
Oh Joy Sex Toy, Pueblo Unido PDX, and *leftycartoons.com*.

IN JUNE OF 2020, I SIGNED A MODELLING CONTRACT.

I HAD BEEN MODELLING FOR YEARS PREVIOUSLY, BUT NEVER THOUGHT IT COULD BE A CAREER DUE TO MY TRANSNESS.

BUT HERE I AM AT 25, MODELLING PROFESSIONALLY.

MY VISIBLE TRANSNESS IS PART OF MY APPEAL.

WHAT HAD MADE SO MANY AGENCIES REJECT ME WAS NOW WHAT PUT ME IN DEMAND.

IT WAS SURREAL, AND BITTERSWEET.

I HAVE SO MUCH FUN WITH MY WORK, AND THE WAY I CONSTANTLY SHIFT MY PRESENTATION ON CAMERA.

I'M PLAYING A ROLE ON CAMERA, BUT I FEEL MORE LIKE MYSELF THAN EVER.

Skylar Swift Kardon
skylarkswift.com

they
he

Skylar Swift Kardon is a mixed transmasculine narrative illustrator. He lives in Los Angeles with his sweet cat Bobbin and a constant flux of foster kittens.

NJ Barna
neonjawboneportfolio.tumblr.com
🐦 @Neonjawbone

she

Nora "NJ" Barna is a transfemme comics powerhouse fueled by a love of hot monsters, mean women, and storytelling.

HILLWALKING IS THE THING I DO TO FIND PEACE. I LIKE THE AIR, THE SPACE, AND BEING HELD BY THE MOUNTAINS. I'M TAKING THE TRANS LIBERATION FLAG UP ALL OF SCOTLAND'S MUNROS, ONE BY ONE.

BUT THE HILLS ARE THE PLACE I WORRY MOST ABOUT PASSING; WITHOUT MAKE-UP, IN FLATTENING OUTDOOR CLOTHES—

HI GIRLS.

"GIRLS"!

"GIRLS"...?

BUT UP HERE, NONE OF THAT MATTERS—

GENDER MELTS AWAY... AND I'M JUST MYSELF.

Harry Josephine Giles
harryjosephine.com
🐦 @HJosephineGiles

they
she

Harry Josephine Giles is a writer and performer from Orkney, living in Leith. Their verse novel *Deep Wheel Orcadia* was published by Picador in October 2021.

art by
Ray Kao
(pg 91)

C. A. P. Ward
artcward.com
🐦 @cevarra

C.A.P. is a black artist working on heartfelt genre stories. Ward is often taking pictures of fungus or skating around Richmond's giant potholes.

Signs

by Harry Josephine Giles

when deep in the landfill the servers awake to weird noises
and diligent winds drop their trade to ask where they're going
and ruminant mountains are steadily making new choices

the screens crack up citywide with the stories they're showing
and circles of well-dressed stones make troubling findings
and couplets and triplets grow strange in the heat of their knowing

but nothing's as queer or as true as a theory unwinding
held in the kinship of ragged and rude-soft voices
the easy and free-tongued choir of the earth and its minding

Other Contributors

Cover Art

C. A. P. Ward
artcward.com
🐦 @cevarra

 they

C.A.P. is a black artist working on heartfelt genre stories. Ward is often taking pictures of fungus or skating around Richmond's giant potholes.

Table of Contents

Ashley Caswell
ashleycaswell.com
🐦 @caswell_ashley

 they

Ashley is a nonbinary illustrator, book designer, and comic artist living in Brooklyn. Their work often explores love, anxiety and growth with a unique sense of humour.

Memory, pg 6

Jay Arthur Simpson
jayarthursimpson.com
🐦 @JayArthurDraws

 he

Jay is an illustrator and mollusc enthusiast from Southwest England.

Discovery, pg 16

G.C. Houle
gchoule.com
🐦 @gchoule

 they

G.C. is a French-Canadian comic artist and graphic designer. They love to tell funny, feel-good stories about queer people, in every sense of the word.

Exploration, pg 24

TOR WAR
torwar.carrd.co
📷 @torwar_

 he

TOR WAR is a Mixed Vietnamese comic creator. He's been trans and happy for the past 3 years, and is looking forward to many more decades to come.

Presentation, pg 34

Rafael G.
rgjelly.portfoliobox.net
📷 @pistachel

 he

Rafael is a Swiss-Portuguese artist whose go-to subjects are queer relationships, supernatural horror and found families with a sprinkle of historical drama.

Acceptance, pg 46

Pa-Luis
pa-luis.wixsite.com/gallery
🐦 @pa__luis

 they

I'm Pa, I traditionally lineart my work and mix it with digital colouring!

Community, pg 54

Ang Hui Qing
anghuiqing.com
🐦 @BurdHQ

 they

Ang Hui Qing is an illustrator and concept artist from Malaysia. Their art seeks to explore the fantastical in the mundane, and the mundane in the fantastical.

Family, pg 62

Val Wise
valkwise.com
🐦 @valkwise

 he

Val Wise is a comic artist based in the Southern US. He contributed to *Rolled & Told*, *Wayward Kindred*, and illustrated *Cheer Up!: Love and Pompoms*.

Intimacy, pg 70

SAINT VAGRANT
198x.love
🐦 @saint_vagrant

 he

Seosamh / SAINT VAGRANT is a bootleg virtual pet. He co-authors the queer sci-fi comic *SUPERPOSE* with his partner Anka.

Freedom, pg 76

Jua OK!
juaok.com
📷 @Jua.ok

 he they

Jua is an illustrator and comic artist whose work explores themes of queer identity, mental illness and relationships using bright colours and fluid line work.

Signs, pg 86

Tzor Edery
basaltbrain.net
📷 @basalt_brain

 they

Tzor is an artist working in multiple fields, including textile and tattoos. Their work centres on queer lives and history, particularly in the Middle East and North Africa.

Other Contributors, pg 88

dairysam
dairysam.wixsite.com/portfolio
📷 @dairy.sam

 they

dairysam is a queer, disabled, brown artist from Toronto. They love playing with colours, shapes and characters to tell stories.

Tamar's Comic, pg 28

Noah Schiatti
behance.net/andrhomeda
🐦 @andrhomeda_

Noah works to depict coming-of-age stories focused on identity and self-acceptance, merging together reality and melancholic dreams.

Peleg's Comic, pg 41

Blop
📷 @le_blop

Hi, I'm Blop, I'm a French trans comic artist that likes to draw webcomics in his free time!

Rotem's Comic, pg 42

Rowan Oats
rowanoats.com

Rowan is a cartoonist from the deep dark woods of Southern Stockholm. They like ducks more than anything.

Ribbons' Comic, pg 52

Jae Zander Kitinoja
jaezander.wixsite.com/portfolio

Jae dreams up comics, short stories, and animated short films. They hope to contribute to the ever-evolving landscape of queer representation.

C-Jay's Comic, pg 59

Tori A. Rielly
toriarie.co
🐦 @toriarie

Tori is a webcomic creator who loves telling stories about queer joy, found family and the long but hopeful process of recovering after difficult experiences.

Josie's Comic, pg 84

Ray Kao
raykaodraws.com

Hi! I'm Ray. I'm a Taiwanese-American artist who focuses on comics and sequential storytelling. I have a passion for books and bugs.

Quindrie Press is an independent comics
publisher based in Edinburgh, Scotland. Our
focus is to provide creators with the opportunity
to publish passion project comics that haven't
found their home anywhere else. We have a
particular interest in helping marginalised and
upcoming creators to publish their work.

Half of all of Quindrie Press' profits from sales
of this book will go towards organisations that
support young transgender people in the UK.

Find more comics at quindriepress.com.